The Winning Team

GEMS MASTERY SERIES

SUCCESS PARADIGMS THAT SEPARATE GOOD TEAMS FROM GREAT TEAMS

Quotes Compiled & Edited

by

DeCarlo A. Eskridge

NU DAE Enterprise Publications

United States of America

ISBN-13: 978-1469932538
ISBN-10: 1469932539

Edited by DeCarlo A. Eskridge
Cover Design ©NU DAE Enterprises, LLC, 2012
DeCarloEskridge.com

Printed in the United States of America

To everyone
who inspires
others to dream,
thank you

Acknowledgments

Jesus (1), Dennis Kinlaw (2, 100), Patanjali (4, 34, 81), Kareem Abdul-Jabbor (5), J. C. Penney (6, 52, 79, 105), Chinese Proverb (7), Henry Ford (8, 45), Ken Blanchard (9), Stephen Covey (10, 47, 95), Helen Keller (11), Michael Jordan (12, 101), Ajaero Tony Martins (13, 115), Sam Walton (14, 113), Vince Lombardi (16, 114), Andrew Carnegie (17), 104), Brian Tracy (18, 85), John Wooden (19), Jack Welch (20, 106), Babe Ruth (21), Mark Sanborn (22, 123), Joe Paterno (23), Tom Landry (24), Tony Dungy (25, 54), Sparky Anderson (26), Ryunosuke Satoro (28), Colin   Powell (29), Lloyd Dobens (30), George Shinn (31), Robert Orben (32), Bill Bradley (33), Robert Reich (35), Golda Meir (36), Benjamin Franklin (37), Norman Shidle (38), Robert Kiyosaki (39), H. E. Luccock (40), Harry S. Truman (41), Lee Iacocca (42, 61), Confucius (43), Jose B.Cabajar (44),AmberHarding (46),Phil Jackson (48), Lewis B. Ergen (49), Duane Hart (50), Max De Pree (51), J. Paul Getty (53), Bill Gates (55), Debra Mancuso (56), Doug Smith (57), W. Edward Deming (58), Althea Gibson (59), Oliver Wendell Holmes (60), DeCarlo A. Eskridge (62, 102), Knute Rockne (63), Dennis Rodman (64), Paul Bear Bryant (65, 124), Bobby Flay (66), Rich Willis (67), Brett Favre (68), Wynton Marsalis (69), Nolan Ryan (70), Virginia Burden (71), Steve Ballmer (72), Dan Marino (73), Shaquille O'Neal (74), Paul Zane Pilzer (75), Mattie Stepanek (76), Margaret Carty (77), Mia Hamm (78), Pat Riley (80), Master Jin Kwon (82), Philip Caldwell (83), B. Dodge (84), Becka Schoettle (86), Michael De Saintamo (87), Robert Kerrigan (88), Bo Schembechler (89), Susan Gale (90), Mark Twain (91), Robert F. Bales (92), Michael Phelps (93), Baltasar Gracion (94),

Latin Maxim (96), Thomas Edison (97), Dr. Rob Gilbert (98), Reinhold Niebuhr (99), Bud Wilkinson (103), John D. Rockefeller (107), Marvin Weisbord (108), John Rollwagen (109), Tom Peters (110), Earvin "Magic" Johnson (111), Richard Branson (112), Bruce Coslet (116), Lou Holtz (117), Napoleon Hill (118), Mike Davidson (119), Tom Wilson (120), Ralph Waldo Emerson (121), Bob Burg (122), Alexander the Great (125)

Introduction

The concept of teamwork is extremely important to the success of any business. Teamwork has the potential to yield some very incredible results. For most of us, teamwork is a part of everyday life. Whether it is at home, in the community, or at work, we are often expected to be a functional part of a performing team.

Teamwork as defined by Webster's New World Dictionary is "a joint action by a group of people, in which each person subordinates his or her individual interests and opinions to the unity and efficiency of the group." Great companies realize that the cultivation of teamwork within their organization is paramount to their survival. The teamwork concept enables individuals to contribute more than they ever thought possible - together. Teamwork: simply stated, it is less me and more we.

In this book, you will discover timeless gems (*quotes*) from some of the world's most influential leaders. Leaders and innovators, who have turned their values into action and, in the process, changed the way the world does business. If you participate in any type of team activities, and/or support anyone in team activities, this book is for you. In order to get the most from this book, we recommend that you read **The Winning Team** until you master the precious gems within.

$\mathcal{O}$f two of you agree...
concerning anything you
desire, it will be done for
you...

- Jesus

♦

*T*eamplayer:

One who unites others
toward a shared destiny
through sharing
information and ideas,
empowering others and
developing trust.

- **Dennis Kinlaw**

◆

T.E.A.M.
Together everyone achieves more.

- Anonymous

◆

When you are inspired by some great purpose, some extraordinary project, all your thoughts break their bonds: Your mind transcends limitations, your consciousness expands in every direction, and you find yourself in a new, great, and wonderful world. Dormant forces, faculties and talents become alive, and your discover yourself to be a greater person by far than you ever dreamed yourself to be.

- Patanjali

One man can be a crucial ingredient on a team, but one man cannot make a team.

- Kareem Abdul-Jabbor

$\mathcal{T}$he best teamwork
comes from men who are
working independently
toward one goal in unison.

- J. C. Penney

◆

Behind every able man,
there are always other able
men.

- Chinese Proverb

$\mathcal{C}$oming together is a
beginning;
keeping together is
progress;
working together is
success.

- Henry Ford

◆

*N*one of us is as smart
as all of us.

- Ken Blanchard

◆

$\mathcal{I}$nterdependent people combine their own efforts with the efforts of others to achieve their greatest success.

- Stephen Covey

♦

$\mathcal{A}$lone we can do so little; together we can do so much.

- Helen Keller

$\mathcal{T}$alent wins games, but teamwork and intelligence wins championships.

- **Michael Jordan**

◆

$\mathcal{O}$f I attack alone, I might turn out to be a wimp. But with a strong business team behind me, I am a force to contend with.

- Ajaero Tony Martins

$\mathcal{W}$e're all working
together;
that's the secret.

– Sam Walton

♦

$\mathcal{N}$etworking is an essential part of building wealth.

- Armstrong Williams

◆

$\mathcal{B}$uild for your team a
feeling of oneness, of
dependence on one another
and of strength to be
derived by unity.

- Vince Lombardi

◆

$\mathcal{T}$eamwork is the ability to work together toward a common vision. The ability to direct individual accomplishments toward organizational objectives. It is the fuel that allows common people to attain uncommon results.

- **Andrew Carnegie**

$\mathcal{T}$eamwork is so important that it is virtually impossible for you to reach the heights of your capabilities or make the money that you want without becoming very good at it.

- Brian Tracy

◆

The main ingredient of stardom is the rest of the team.

- John Wooden

The team with the best
players wins.

- Jack Welch

The way a team plays as a whole determines its success. You may have the greatest bunch of individual stars in the world, but if they don't play together, the club won't be worth a dime.

- **Babe Ruth**

♦

In teamwork, silence
isn't golden, it's deadly.

- Mark Sanborn

◆

When a team outgrows individual performance and learns team confidence, excellence becomes a reality.

- Joe Paterno

♦

$\mathcal{I}$don't believe in team motivation. I believe in getting a team prepared so it knows it will have the necessary confidence when it steps on a field and be prepared to play a good game.

- Tom Landry

♦

The secret to success is good leadership, and good leadership is all about making the lives of your team members or workers better.

- Tony Dungy

◆

We're the best team in
baseball,
but not by much.

- Sparky Anderson

◆

Winning teams beat with one heart.

- Michelle Campbell

◆

Individually,
we are one drop.
Together,
we are an ocean.

- Ryunosuke Satoro
♦

When we are debating an issue, loyalty means giving me your honest opinion, whether you think I'll like it or not. Disagreement, at this stage, stimulates me. But once a decision has been made, the debate ends. From that point on, loyalty means executing the decision as if it were your own.

- Colin Powell

$\mathcal{I}$t is not a question of how well each process works, the question is how well they all work together.

- **Lloyd Dobens**

♦

There is no such thing as a self-made man.
You will reach your goals only with the help of others.

- George Shinn

♦

$\mathcal{I}$f you can laugh together, you can work together.

- **Robert Orben**

$\mathcal{R}$espect your fellow human being, treat them fairly, disagree with them honestly, enjoy their friendship, explore your thoughts about one another candidly, work together for a common goal and help one another achieve it.

- Bill Bradley

When a gifted team
dedicates itself to unselfish
trust and combines instinct
with boldness and effort,
it is ready to climb.

- Patanjali

◆

$\mathcal{Y}$our most precious possession is not your financial assets. Your most precious possession is the people you have working there, and what they carry around in their heads, and their ability to work together.

- Robert Reich

I never did anything alone. Whatever was accomplished in this country was accomplished collectively.

- **Golda Meir**

♦

$\mathcal{W}$e must all hang together or most assuredly we shall hang separately.

- **Benjamin Franklin**

◆

$\mathcal{A}$ group becomes a team when each member is sure enough of himself and his contribution to praise the skills of the others.

- Norman Shidle

♦

The richest people in the world look for and build networks. Everyone else looks for work.

- Robert Kiyosaki

♦

No one can whistle a symphony. It takes a whole orchestra to play it.

- H. E. Luccock

♦

$\mathcal{I}$t is amazing how much you can accomplish when it doesn't matter who gets the credit.

- **Harry S. Truman**

◆

$\mathcal{A}$ major reason capable people fail to advance is that they don't work well with their colleagues.

- Lee Iacocca

◆

When you meet someone better than yourself, turn your thoughts to becoming his equal. When you meet someone not as good as you are, look within and examine your own self.

- Confucius

♦

There is no such thing as "one-man show" in a winning team.

- Jose B. Cabajar

♦

$\mathcal{I}$f everyone is moving forward together, then success takes care of itself.

- Henry Ford

♦

$\mathcal{C}$ontrary to popular belief, there most certainly IS an "I" in TEAM. It is the same "I" that appears 3 times in RESPONSIBILITY.

- Amber Harding

♦

Strength lies in
differences,
not in similarities.

- Stephen Covey

♦

The strength of the team is each individual member…the strength of each member is the team.

- Phil Jackson

♦

The ratio of "We's" to "I's" is the best indicator of the development of a team.

- Lewis B. Ergen

◆

Teamwork divides the task and doubles the success.

- Duane Hart

◆

The key elements in the art of working together are how to deal with change, how to deal with conflict, and how to reach our potential...the needs of the team are best met when we meet the needs of individual persons.

- Max De Pree

♦

$\mathcal{D}$o not primarily train men to work. Train them to serve willingly and intelligently.

- J. C. Penney

♦

$\mathcal{I}$'d rather have one percent of the efforts of 100 people than 100 percent of my own efforts.

- J. Paul Getty

♦

$\mathcal{Y}$ou need togetherness because you don't always win, and you have got to hang though together.

- Tony Dungy

♦

$\mathcal{T}$eams should be able to act with the same unity of purpose and focus as a well motivated individual.

- Bill Gates

♦

$\mathcal{W}$in together,
lose together,
play together,
stay together.

- Debra Mancuso

$\mathcal{T}$eams share the burden
and divide the grief.

- Doug Smith

◆

What we need to do is learn to work in the system, by which I mean that everybody, every team, every platform, every division, every component is there not for individual competitive profit or recognition, but for contribution to the system as a whole on a win-win basis.

- W. Edward Deming

◆

$\mathcal{N}$o matter what accomplishments you make, somebody helped you.

- Althea Gibson

◆

$\mathcal{I}$won't accept anything less than the best a player's capable of doing... and he has the right to expect the best that I can do for him and the team!

- Oliver Wendell Holmes

♦

I've always found that
the speed of the boss
is the speed of the team.

- Lee Iacocca

♦

$\mathcal{S}$uccess is not finding
the right people,
but becoming the right
person.

- DeCarlo A. Eskridge

The secret is to work less as individuals and more as a team.

- Knute Rockne

◆

The NBA believes if you play for a team and get paid by a team, you're the property of that team for 24 hours a day.

- Dennis Rodman

♦

$\mathcal{A}$ good, quick, small team can beat a big, slow team any time.

- Paul Bear Bryant

There are so many great
things about this business.
Almost everybody is on
the same team.
It is all for one-friendly
competitiveness. No one is
out to hurt anyone.

- Bobby Flay

◆

*W*henever ideas are shared, the result is always greater than the sum of the parts.

- Rich Willis

◆

It's not a one man team win or lose.

- Brett Favre

You need a team.
You need people to push
you. You need opponents.

- Wynton Marsalis

♦

$\mathcal{M}$y job is to give my team a chance to win.

- Nolan Ryan

◆

$\mathcal{C}$ooperation is the
thorough conviction that
nobody can get there
unless everybody gets
there.

- Virginia Burden

◆

$\mathcal{A}$ll companies of any size have to continue to push to make sure you get the right leaders, the right team, the right people to be fast acting, and fast moving in the marketplace. We've got great leaders, and we continue to attract and promote great new leaders.

- Steve Ballmer

◆

It's real nice and
exciting for me to break
the records,
but it's more exciting for
me to be on a winning
team.

- **Dan Marino**

♦

This is the right place,
the right time,
the right team.

- Shaquille O'Neal

◆

You only win when you help others win.

- Paul Zane Pilzer

♦

$\mathcal{U}$nity is strength;
when there is teamwork
and collaboration,
wonderful things can be
achieved.

- Mattie Stepanek

◆

The nice thing about teamwork is that you always have others on your side.

- Margaret Carty

◆

I am a member of a team, and I rely on the team, I defer to it and sacrifice for it, because the team, not the individual, is the ultimate champion.

- Mia Hamm

♦

The five separate fingers
are five independent units.
Close them and the fist
multiplies strength.
This is organization.

- J. C. Penney

♦

$\mathcal{G}$reat teamwork is the only way we create the breakthroughs that define our careers.

- Pat Riley

◆

When a gifted team
dedicates itself to unselfish
trust and combines instinct
with boldness and effort,
it is ready to climb.

- Patanjali

♦

$\mathcal{O}$ne piece of log creates a small fire, adequate to warm you up, add just a few more pieces to blast an immense bonfire, large enough to warm up your entire circle of friends; needless to say that individuality counts but team work dynamites.

- Master Jin Kwon

◆

The important thing to recognize is that it takes a team, and the team ought to get credit for the wins and the losses. Successes have many fathers, failures have none.

- Philip Caldwell

♦

$\mathcal{N}$o problem
is insurmountable.
With a little courage,
teamwork,
and determination
a person can overcome
anything.

- B. Dodge

♦

$\mathcal{T}$eamwork is so important that it is virtually impossible for you to reach the heights of your capabilities or make the money that you want without becoming very good at it.

- Brian Tracy

◆

*C*ogether,
ordinary people can
achieve extraordinary
results.

- Becka Schoettle

◆

When two people meet, there are really six people present. There is each man as he sees himself, each man as he wants to be seen, and each man as he really is.

- Michael De Saintamo

♦

The way of the world
is meeting people through
other people.

- Robert Kerrigan

♦

When your team is winning, be ready to be tough, because winning can make you soft. On the other hand, when your team is losing, stick by them. Keep believing.

- **Bo Schembechler**

◆

*N*ever be content to sit on the sidelines when there is so much work to be done on the field.

- Susan Gale

♦

Synergy — the bonus that is achieved when things work together harmoniously.

- **Mark Twain**

♦

ffective teamwork will not take the place of knowing how to do the job or how to manage the work. Poor teamwork, however, can prevent effective final performance. And it can also prevent team members from gaining satisfaction in being a member of a team and the organization.

- Robert F. Bales

I always thought,
it would be neat to make
the Olympic team.

- Michael Phelps

♦

The path to greatness is along with others.

- Baltasar Gracion

♦

Synergy is the highest
activity of life; it creates
new untapped alternatives;
it values and exploits the
mental, emotional, and
psychological differences
between people.

- Stephen Covey

♦

Æ Pluribus Unum —
Out of many, one.

- Latin Maxim

♦

If I could solve all the
problems myself,
I would.

- Thomas Edison

*W*orking together
works.

- Dr. Rob Gilbert

Men have never been
individually self-sufficient.

- Reinhold Niebuhr

◆

Work and self-worth are the two factors in pride that interact with each other and that tend to increase the strong sense of pride found in superior work teams. When people do something of obvious worth, they feel a strong sense of personal worth.

- Dennis Kinlaw

♦

There is no "i" in team
but there is in win.

- Michael Jordan

◆

$\mathcal{G}$od answers the prayers of the better-prepared team.

- DeCarlo A. Eskridge

$\mathcal{I}$f a team is to reach its potential, each player must be willing to subordinate his personal goals to the good of the team.

- **Bud Wilkinson**

♦

Mr. J. P. Morgan buys
his partners,
I grow my own.

- Andrew Carnegie

◆

$\mathcal{M}$y definition of an executive's job is brief and straight to the point. It's simply this: Getting things done through other people.

- J. C. Penney

◆

$\mathcal{I}$f you pick the right people and give them the opportunity to spread their wings and put compensation as a carrier behind it, you almost don't have to manage them.

- Jack Welch

♦

$\mathcal{G}$ood leadership consists of showing average people how to do the work of superior people.

- John D. Rockefeller

*T*eamwork
is the quintessential
contradiction of a society
grounded in individual
achievement.

- Marvin Weisbord

◆

$\mathcal{W}$e have always found that people are most productive in small teams with tight budgets, time lines and the freedom to solve their own problems.

- John Rollwagen

The leaders who work most effectively, it seems to me, never say 'I'. They don't think 'I'. They think 'we'; they think 'team'.

- Tom Peters

♦

Everybody on a championship team doesn't get publicity, but everyone can say he's a champion.

- Earvin "Magic" Johnson

◆

$\mathcal{T}$o be successful, you have to be out there, you have to hit the ground running, and if you have a good team around you and more than a fair share of luck, you might make something happen. But you certainly can't guarantee it just by following someone else's formula.

- **Richard Branson**

♦

*Individuals
don't win in business,
teams do.*

- Sam Walton

$\mathcal{T}$eams do not go
physically flat,
they go mentally stale.

- Vince Lombardi

♦

Go to the wolf, consider its ways and be wise. A wolf will never hunt alone; it hunts in packs because it knows the power of team work.

- **Ajaero Tony Martins**

The era of the rugged individual is giving way to the era of the team player. Everyone is needed, but no one is necessary.

- Bruce Coslet

◆

$\mathcal{A}$ll winning teams are goal-oriented. Teams like these win consistently because everyone connected with them concentrates on specific objectives. They go about their business with blinders on; nothing will distract them from achieving their aims.

- Lou Holtz

♦

The best job goes to the person who can get it done without passing the buck or coming back with excuses.

- Napoleon Hill

♦

It's all about people. It's about networking and being nice to people and not burning any bridges.

- Mike Davidson

$\mathcal{M}$any of us are more capable than some of us; but none of us is as capable as all of us.

- Tom Wilson

◆

$\mathcal{T}$rust men and they will be true to you; treat them greatly, and they will show themselves great.

- Ralph Waldo Emerson

The successful networkers I know, the ones receiving tons of referrals and feeling truly happy about themselves, continually put the other person's needs ahead of their own.

- Bob Burg

♦

The greatest danger a team faces isn't that it won't become successful, but that it will, and then cease to improve.

- Mark Sanborn

♦

In order to have a
winner, the team must have
a feeling of unity;
every player must put the
team first-ahead of
personal glory.

- Paul Bear Bryant

◆

$\mathscr{R}$emember upon the conduct of each depends the fate of all.

- Alexander the Great

About the Author

DeCarlo A. Eskridge is a spiritual life-coach/trainer, host of Blogtalk Radio's "Live Your Greatness," motivational speaker, certified hypnotherapist, certified N.L.P. practitioner/trainer, author, business owner, and minister. He is very proud to have authored and independently-published several books through his company NU DAE Enterprises where he serves as President and CEO.

A prolific teacher and encourager, DeCarlo A. Eskridge reads over 50 books a year, and listens to countless hours of audio programs. He is a Certified Life Coach through Franklin Covey and a motivational speaker who earned advanced honors at Toastmasters International. He is also an Ordained Minister with over 25 years of biblical study.

DeCarlo A. Eskridge has been imbued with an inexhaustible, unyielding, and unrelenting thirst and hunger for knowledge. His mission is to travel the globe teaching, empowering, inspiring, and transforming the lives of millions with the truths he has discovered in order that every person recognizes who he or she is, what he or she can accomplish, and that they live it!

GEMS MASTERY SERIES

NU DAE Enterprise Publications

DeCarloEskridge.com

ISBN-13: 978-1469932538
ISBN-10: 1469932539